SOUNDS LiKE READiNG
BOOK EIGHT

The Clown in the Gown Drives the Car with the Star

A BOOK ABOUT DIPHTHONGS AND R-CONTROLLED VOWELS

Brian P. Cleary

illustrations by
Jason Miskimins

Consultant:
Alice M. Maday
Ph.D. in Early Childhood Education with a Focus in Literacy
Assistant Professor, Retired
Department of Curriculum and Instruction
University of Minnesota

M Millbrook Press/Minneapolis

to Miss Gasper,
my seventh-grade teacher in Rocky River, Ohio
—B.P.C.

Millbrook Press
A division of Lerner Publishing Group, Inc.
241 First Avenue North
Minneapolis, MN 55401 U.S.A.

Website address: www.lernerbooks.com

Library of Congress Cataloging-in-Publication Data

Cleary, Brian P., 1959–
    The clown in the gown drives the car with the star : a book about diphthongs
and r-controlled vowels / by Brian P. Cleary ; illustrations by Jason Miskimins ;
consultant Alice M. Maday, Ph.D.
        p.   cm. — (Sounds like reading)
    ISBN 978–0–8225–7637–2 (lib. bdg. : alk. paper)
    1. English language—Vowels—Juvenile literature. 2. English language—
Consonants—Juvenile literature. 3. English language—Phonetics—Juvenile
literature. 4. Reading—Phonetic method—Juvenile literature. I. Miskimins,
Jason, ill. II. Maday, Alice M. III. Title.
PE1157.C543 2009
428.1—dc22   2008025477

Manufactured in the United States of America
2 – PC – 8/1/09

Dear Parents and Educators,

As a former adult literacy coach and the father of three children, I know that learning to read isn't always easy. That's why I developed **Sounds Like Reading**®—a series that uses a combination of devices to help children learn to read.

This book is the eighth in the **Sounds Like Reading**® series. It uses rhyme, repetition, illustration, and phonics to introduce young readers to diphthongs—vowel sound combinations in which the sound of one letter glides into the other, as in t*oy*—and r-controlled vowels—vowels in which the sound changes because of the presence of the r, such as the *a* in *star*.

Starting on page 4, you'll see three rhyming words on each left-hand page. These words are part of the sentence on the facing page. They all feature a diphthong or an r-controlled vowel. As the book progresses, the sentences become more challenging. These sentences contain a "discovery" word—an extra rhyming word in addition to those that appear on the left. Toward the end of the book, the sentences contain two discovery words. And for an extra challenge, the final sentence in this book contains three! Children will delight in the increased confidence that finding and decoding the discovery words will bring. They'll also enjoy looking for the mouse that appears throughout the book. The mouse asks readers to look for words that sound alike.

The bridge to literacy is one of the most important we will ever cross. It is my hope that the **Sounds Like Reading**® series will help young readers to hop, gallop, and skip from one side to the other!

Sincerely,

Brian P. Cleary

Look for me to help you find the words that sound alike!

oil

foil

soil

Can you find three words that sound alike?

He poured **oil** on the **foil** on the **soil**.

saw

paw

jaw

Can you find three words that sound alike?

I **saw** her **paw** on his **jaw**.

mouse

blouse

house

Can you find three words that sound alike?

The **mouse** took the **blouse** from her **house**.

herd

bird

third

Can you find three words that sound alike?

The **herd** and the **bird** finished **third**.

There is **tar** on the **car** in the shape of a **star**.

bow

mow

row

Can you find three words that sound alike?

14

The girl with the **bow** will **mow** grass in a **row**.

cow

plow

chow

The **cow** by the **plow** will eat her **chow now**.

Can you find the word that sounds like cow, plow, and chow?

clown

gown

crown

Can you find the word that sounds like clown, gown, and crown?

18

The **clown** in the **gown** has a **brown crown**.

Bert

skirt

shirt

Can you find the word that sounds like Bert, skirt, and shirt?

Bert got **dirt** on her **skirt** and **shirt**.

squares

chairs

stairs

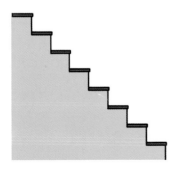

Can you find the word that sounds like squares, chairs, and stairs?

22

He **stares** at the **squares** on the **chairs** by the **stairs**.

crow

throw

snow

Can you find the word that sounds like crow, throw, and snow?

The **slow crow** can **throw snow**.

Troy

boy

toy

TOYS

Can you find two words that sound like Troy, boy, and toy?

Joy and **Roy** gave **Troy** and his **boy** a **toy**.

scout

trout

spout

Can you find two words that sound like scout, trout, and spout?

28

The **scout** had to **shout** when he looked **out** and saw a **trout** with a **spout**.

cook

hook

book

Can you find three words that sound like cook, hook, and book?

The **cook** with the **hook took** a **look** at the **book** in his **nook**.